GW01463860

Mick McFall
The Mythical Man

Compiled and Edited
by
Graham Hopner

Illustrations by Zoë Hopner

Blackhouseland Publishers
1996

Published by Blackhouseland Publishers, Balloch.
Typeset by Castle Danger Press, Alexandria.
Printed by Clydeside Printers, Glasgow.

ISBN 0-9528852-0-4

Contents

Introduction

Dumbarton and the Vale of Leven have had a good share of worthies -
Dougal the Cratur, Wee Dick Ponsonby, Popeye and the Road Runner, but
most were unusual for some character trait or physical peculiarity. None has
left behind him such a rich trail of sayings and jokes, or "baurs," as did Mick
McFall. It is now almost impossible to distinguish between what he said and
what has been made up in his name. Indeed many people who have heard of
him are not sure if he is a real or fictional character. Probably many of the
Irishisms attributed to him, such as "hauf o the lies he tells is true," do come
from Mick, but most of the jokes come from other people after he had
achieved local vaudeville popularity.

Mick is claimed as a native of most of the villages in the Vale of Leven and
even of Clydebank, but the people who knew him personally attest to his
being from Dumbarton. In fact he was born in Ireland, most likely in
Portglenone to the west of Ballymena in County Antrim, in 1875 or 1876,
the 7th of 8 children of Eanis McFall and Mary Birnie. Mick's oldest brother
and sisters were born in Portglenone, but the Registrar General in Dublin has
no birth certificate for Mick in this parish, which suggests that he was born
elsewhere in Ireland, or perhaps he was born in Portglenone but for some
reason the event went unregistered. Mick's father brought the family over to
Dumbarton around 1880 and got a job in Hardie & Gordon's foundry at
Dalreoch, next to the Dennystown Forge.

According to a co-worker, John Reilly, an engineer at Drysdale's Pumps,
Mick followed his father and served his time at Hardie & Gordon's, but
worked most of his life as a brass and iron dresser at Bull's Metal and
Metalloid Company in Bulldale Street, Yoker. His brother Dennis and
nephew Charles worked there with him as iron dressers.

In 1897 Mick was living at 18 Hall Street, Renton, when on the last day of
the year he married Sarah Perrie, a printfield hand, probably in Cordale or
Dalquhurn textile works, at 'The Chapel,' Our Lady and St Mark's, then in
North Street, Alexandria.

On the last day of May 1898 a son Eanis was born at 18 Levenbank Street in Dennystown, Dumbarton. Sadly the boy died of meningitis at the age of 15 months at 35 William Street. There do not appear to have been any more children to this marriage, and it would seem that Mick and Sarah parted. Fifteen years later, in September 1913, Sarah died of TB in the Joint Fever Hospital on Cardross Road. According to her death certificate, which was signed by her brother-in-law James Buntine, Sarah had been a domestic servant at Station Cottage, Longriddry, East Lothian. The certificate was prepared under the supervision of the registrar William Weymark, father of another of the town's characters, Freddy (" Time on your watch?") Weymark.

Next year, 1914, Mick was living at 16 Levenbank Street in Dennystown, a part of the town he never left. At the end of the war he was at 20 George Street. He is described in the voters rolls as an iron dresser, which is what others always called him, but he always called himself a brass dresser.

In July 1916 his mother died of a stroke at the Little Sisters Home in Greenock, where she had been taken from her house in Levenbank Street. Her husband had died at Larbert Asylum in June 1905.

At the end of the First World War Mick picked himself up and remarried, his second wife a young widow seventeen years younger than him. Mary Boyd, a printfield worker, had married Alan Foster, a forge labourer, in February 1914 in accordance with Free Church rites. A girl Annie was born in Mary's home, 22 Henryshott. Her husband seems to have gone missing in the War.

On the 7th November 1919 Mick and Mary married in St Patrick's Chapel in Strathleven Place. Mick moved from the model lodging house in Risk Street to Mary's house at 17 Levenhaugh Street, his home for the rest of his life. Six children were born here: Margaret in July 1921, Bridget Boyd in November 1923, Michael in November 1924, Mary in February 1927, Jane Boyd in July 1929 and Teresa in August 1931. It was in this period that Mick seems to have started to become well known.

It would appear that Mick's funny way of talking "kind o airse aboot face" gained a certain popularity in the 1920s, and he was credited with sayings such as:

"You fellahs are always the same sometimes."

"The auld songs are the best - they ought tae write mair o them!"

"Everything in mah favour's against me."

"Ah never hit mah weans except in self-defence."

Towards the end of the 1920s, probably as a by-product of unemployment caused by the Depression, local cinemas and theatres put on local talent shows called Go As You Please shows. Sometimes they would be held in between films, sometimes on special evenings. For a few pence you could enter and put your name on the programme, and there would be three winners, getting prizes of, say, thirty shillings, a pound and ten shillings.

One of Mick's friends was Tim Martin, a member of a comedy duo known as Barclay and Martin who appeared regularly in these Go As You Please contests, and Tim began to impersonate Mick as part of the act. People can remember seeing Mick watching himself being "done" in at least one of the shows, and he seems to have enjoyed his local notoriety, and even started playing up to it a bit. In the 1930s and 1940s a whole corpus of McFallisms grew up, and survive to this day, having been passed down to us through the generations.

According to Jim Adie, who can recall seeing Mick outside the Black Bull just before the Second World War, he was then an oldish man with white and grey flecked hair but a fresh complexion, despite the wrinkles. On another occasion Jim noticed that Mick had a prominent gap in his front teeth. He was by now consciously contributing to his own immortalising. He would hear jokes and retell them, adding himself as one of the characters. As well as enjoying his fame Mick was in all probability deliberately playing a subtle game, posing as the simple Irishman, but at the same time feeding material to, and so manipulating, his deriders.

The war jokes relating to Mick seem to refer to both World Wars. He did indeed live through both wars... just! Two days after VE Day and the end of World War 2, on 10th May 1945, Mick died in, of all places, Dumfries. He died like his mother before him of a stroke, in Galloway House. Was he on holiday? If he was, it's not certain he had taken his wife with him. A. Campbell, the occupier, signed his death certificate, maybe from information supplied by his second wife Mary, who survived him by nearly 30 years. She lived latterly with her son Michael at 7A Stonyflatt Road in Bellsmyre, dying in February 1974.

Mick left behind him a swathe of jokes, set between Balloch and Clydebank and even extending at times to Paisley, Glasgow and Helensburgh, including many later creations set against events that occurred after his death, such as the closing of Denny's and the establishment of the nuclear submarine base at Faslane. Proof that his humour is timeless and is adapted to contemporary life in the eternal fascination with jokes. A lot of material on Mick was collected by Gordon McCulloch for the School of Scottish Studies and published in their magazine Tocher in 1983. Information was supplied by James McGroggan and other pensioners, and Jim Kearns of St Patrick's High School.

I have here published all jokes and sayings I have been able to collect. I have not acted as critic or censor, so there may be material which is poor, or at least poor in taste. I have only picked up the bits I could find of what Mick McFall had left behind.

Graham Hopner
Compiler and Editor

Acknowledgments

I should like to thank the following for supplying me with jokes by and information on Mick McFall:

Jim Adie, Jeannie Arkinstall, Margaret Brand,
Tom Gallacher, Peter Graham, Robert Graham,
Arthur Jones, William Jones, Jim Kearns,
John Kennedy, Malcolm Lobban, Gordon McCulloch,
Eddie McGhie, Bob McGregor, James McGroggan,
Tommy Poole, John Reilly, John Strathearn,
and St. Patrick's High School IC class of 1981-82;
also the Lennox Herald for permission to reproduce from
their edition of 10 July 1926, and New Register House
for permission to reproduce the 1881 and 1891
Dumbarton census entries: Crown copyright is
reproduced with the permission of HMSO.

The Pedigree of Mick McFall.
The McFall Family in Dumbarton from County Antrim.
(Note there are several other familes named McFall in Dumbarton).

Margaret McFall	Dennis McFall	Mary Ann McFall	Sarah McFall
b. 13/1/1864	Iron Dresser	b. 13/6/1867	Printfield Worker,
Port Glenone, Antrim	b. 24/5/1865	Port Glenone,	in Dumbarton 1891
She was witness	PortGlenone, Antrim	Antrim.	b. 1869-1870 Ireland
to the marriage of	m. Catherine Corcoran 1887		
her brother Dennis	daughter of Patrick Corcoran & Ann Cunningham		
in 1887	b. 1867 Ireland		
	Both residing at 13 Levenbank Street Dumbarton 1891.		
	Dennis was then employed as an Iron Foundry labourer.		
	Mary and Bridget Corcoran, her sisters, were lodgers		
	with them in 1891.		

Mary Ann McFall	Dennis McFall	Catherine McFall	Charles McFall	Margaret McFall
b. c1887	b. 28/11/1888	Residing in Partick 1989	Iron Dresser	b. 1901 Dumbarton
Dumbarton	Dumbarton	b1890-91 Dumbarton		d. 26/3/1990 aged 88
		d. December 1989 aged 98		m. John 'Sonny' Hendry 1921
		m. to ..... Keenan		Railway Porter at Dumbarton East
		Uncle of Peter Keenan the Boxer		

Bertha Hendry	John Hendry	Catherine Hendry	Gerald Hendry	Margaret Hendry
b	b.	b.	b.	b.
m.	m.	m.	m.	m.
Ced......Tapley		...McGall	Catherine Arnold	Donald Brand
				12 Round Riding Rd.

(Child by First Marriage)   (Step daughter of Mick McFall)

Eanis McFall	Annie Foster	Margaret McFall	Bridget Boyd McFall
b. 31/5/1898 Dumbarton	b. 22/3/1914	b. 31/7/1921	b. 13/11/1923
d. 7/9/1899 Dumbarton	Dumbarton.	Dumbarton	Dumbarton

James McFall, (farmer in Antrim.)
Married to Margaret Munn.

Eneas /Eanis (Dennis) McFall,
Came to Scotland from Ireland about 1880
b. in Ireland approx 1825 -1833
Lived at 16 Levenbank Street Dumbarton in 1891
d. 14/6/1905 at Larbert
m. 1st. to Janet Donnelly
m. 2nd. to Mary Birnie
daughter of Denis Birnie & Mary Ann McNaughton
b. 1834 - 1838 in Ireland
d. 22 Aug. 1916 in Greenock.

Jane McFall	James McFall	**Michael McFall**	Felix McFall
Printfield Worker	Apprentice Iron Moulder	Gen. Labourer in Dumbarton 1891	Scholar in 1891
in Dumbarton 1891	in Dumbarton 1891	Iron/Brass Dresser in 1914 - 1918	Metal Carrier.
b. 1871-1872	b. 1873-1874 Ireland	b. 1875-1876 Ireland	in Brassworks
Ireland	m. Isabella McGinlay	d. 10/5/1945 Dumfries	b. 1877-1879 Ire.
	29/6/1917 Dumbarton	**m. 1st to Sarah Perrie**	d.
		31/12/1897 Alexandria	m. Rebecca Goldie
	Eneas McFall	daughter of Francis Perrie	11/7/1918 in
	Acetylene Cutter in Denny's	& Ruth Andrews	Dumbarton.
	b. 12/10/1921 Dumbarton	b 9/6/1876 Dumbarton	
	m. Sarah Heaney	d. 27/9/1913 Dumbarton	
	6/6/1947 Dumbarton	**m. 2nd to Mary Boyd,**	
		who also married Alan Foster,	
	Thomas McFall	as her 1st husband on 23/2/1914	
	Burner in Scotts of Bowling	daughter of Daniel Boyd & Bridget O'Donnell	
	b. 1948 Dumbarton	b. 13/1/1889 or 1892/93 Ireland	
		d. 6/2/1974 Dumbarton	

Ninnie McFall	Christine McFall	Isabella McFall
b.	b.	b.
m.	m.	m.
d.	d.	d.
Tony Perelli	Joseph Perelli	Patrick Costello

Dennis Hendry	Mary Hendry	Josephine Hendry
b.	b.	b.
m.	m.	m.
	.. Buchanan	
	in High Mains D'ton	

Michael McFall	**Mary McFall**	**Jane Boyd McFall**	**Teresa McFall**
b. 8/11/1924	b. 22/2/1927	b. 1/7/1929	b. 15/8/1931
Dumbarton	Dumbarton	Dumbarton	Dumbarton

The Young Immigrant.

A five-year-old Michael McFall is a 'visitor' at 70 Levenhaugh Street, overlooking the River Leven, at the time of the 1881 census. With him are his brothers Felix(3), James (7), and his sisters Jane (9), Sarah (11), and his mother Mary.

				The undermentioned Houses are
Civil Parish of *Cardross*	Quod Sacra Parish of *Dalreoch*	School Board District of *Burgh of Dumbarton*		Parliamentary Burgh of *Dumbarton*

No of Schedule	Road, Street, &c., and No. and Name of House.	Houses In habited	Unin habited	Name and Surname of each Person	Relation to Head of Family
4	70 Levenhaugh St.	1		John Neeson	Head
	Part of Henryshott.			Daniel Neeson	Brother
				Patrick Neeson	Son
				Elizabeth Kerr	Ho. Keeper
				Elizabeth Kerr	do Daughter
				Mary McFall	Visitor
				Sarah do	do
				Jane do	do
				James do	do
				Michael do	do
				Felix do	do

More Settled Times

A teenage Michael McFall in 16 Levenbank Street at the time of the 1891 census. Father Eanis ('Dennis') has joined his wife and five children.

Page 30					The undermentioned Houses a
	Civil Parish of *Cardross*	Quod Sacra Parish of *Dalreoch*		School Board District of *Dumbarton*	
	Municipal Burgh of	Police Burgh of *Dumbarton*		Burgh Ward of	

No of Schedule	Road, Street, &c., and No. and Name of House.	Houses In habited	Unin habited	Name and Surname of each Person	Relation to Head of Family	Condition as to Marriage
142	70 Levenbank St.			Dennis McFall	Head	Married
				Mary do	Wife	Married
				Sarah do	Daur	Unm
				Jane do	Daur	Unm
				James do	Son	Unm
				Michael do	Son	
				Felix do	Son	

They are all 'visiting' the brothers John and Daniel Neeson, Daniel's son Patrick and the housekeeper Elizabeth Kerr and her daughter Elizabeth. All eleven persons are living in one room!

situate within the Boundaries of the

Royal Burgh of			Police Burgh of *Dumbarton*	Town of *Dumbarton*	Village or Hamlet of **40**	
Condition as to Marriage	Age Males	Age Females	Rank, Profession, Occupation.	Where Born	1. Deaf and Dumb 2. Blind 3. Lunatic Imbecile 4. Idiot	No of Rooms with Windows
Widower	54		Shipyard Labourer	Ireland		1
Married	41		Gardener's do	do		
	3			Dunbartonshire, Cardross		
Widow		45	Housekeeper	Ireland		
		14	Printfield Worker	Dunbartonshire, Dumbarton		
Married		46	Forge labourer's Wife	Ireland		
		11	do Daur	do		
		9	do Daur	do		
	7		do Son	do		
	5		do Son	do		
	3		do Son	do		

The fourteen-year-old Michael is described as a general labourer, and the family are now living in the comparative luxury of two rooms.

situate within the Boundaries of the

			Parliamentary Burgh of *Dumbarton*				Parliamentary Division of	Royal Burgh of		
			Town of *Dumbarton*				Village or Hamlet of	Island of		
Age Males	Age Females		Rank, Profession, Occupation.	Employer	Employed	Self Employed	Where Born	Gaelic or G & E	1. Deaf and Dumb 2. Blind 3. Lunatic or imbecile 4. Idiot	No of Rooms with Windows
65			Labourer in Iron Foundry		X		Ireland			2
	56						do			
	20		Printfield Worker		X		do			
	18		do do		X		do			
16			Apprentice Moulder		X		do			
14			General labourer		X		do			
12			Scholar				do			

No joke - Mick Crashes

One of the few first hand accounts of events in Mick McFall's life is this newspaper report of a bus crash - by which time the 50 year-old believes himself to be 47 !

CARDROSS ROAD BUS SMASH

A DOUBLE-DECKER OVERTURNS. - LIST OF INJURED.

Lennox Herald
July 10, 1926.

An alarming bus smash, happily unattended by fatality, although about forty persons were more or less injured, occurred on the Cardross-Dumbarton Road, near Ardoch, on Saturday evening. The bus involved was one of the London, double-decked type, weighing in itself about 5 tons, and with a carrying capacity of 54 passengers. This type was the first put on the local roads by Dumbarton General Omnibus Company, Ltd., and has proved the popular fine weather bus, with their outside seats on the top deck. The bus in question had left Helensburgh on its run to Dumbarton, and had on board a full complement of passengers, among whom were a party comprising members of a Dumbarton Boys' Brigade Company, with girl friends, who joined at Ardmore. At Ardoch there are two bends on the roadway. The first of these was negotiated quite safely. This one goes to the left, and is followed by a straight stretch of about 100 yards. Then the bend where the accident took place was reached, the road turning to the right. For some reason yet unexplained, in rounding the bus got in contact with the kerb on the right-hand side of the road. It ran along for over twenty yards, it is understood, practically on two wheels. Then it got onto the soft ground inside the kerb, glanced along a stone dyke about three feet high, tearing the dyke on its way before overturning on its side on the roadway. The upper-deck passengers were thrown in a heap on to the road, while those inside were imprisoned amid the shattered glass. The scene was one of general confusion, several of the passengers lying injured and unconscious. It was marvellous how everyone escaped with their lives. The passengers inside were soon rescued by those unhurt or with slight injury; the evening being fine and there being still daylight, the work of the rescuers was rendered the more easy. The traffic on the road was also fairly busy, and help came from all quarters. Several doctors were soon on the scene, as well as ladies with nursing experience. Dumbarton Burgh Ambulance was phoned for and arrived promptly. In it and in buses and private cars sixteen people were conveyed to Dumbarton Cottage Hospital, where their injuries were attended to by Drs Robertson and Humble and Miss Galbraith and her staff of nurses. Here it was found necessary to detain for treatment only three persons. Patrick Lynch, the driver of the bus, suffered from severe shock; Mrs Hannah, a dislocation of the left elbow, fractured left wrist and bruised hip; and Michael McFall, injury to the right leg and a cut on the right side of the head.

As the bus was lying on the roadway blocking the traffic, willing hands worked planks as levers and edged it out of the way so that other traffic managed past by mounting the opposite pavement. Later in the evening a squad of riggers from Messrs McMillan's Dockyard appeared on the scene with necessary tackle and got the vehicle back on its wheels, when it was towed to the depot in Dumbarton.

A passenger who was riding on the platform of the capsized bus described his experience as terrible. To have jumped off would have meant serious injury. This same gentleman's opinion was that had the bus overturned over the wall, fatalities would certainly have been numerous, as there is a drop, and many would have been crushed. Another gentleman who with his wife was travelling on the second front seat of the upper deck, described the confusion among the passengers as terrible during the short distance the bus ran on two wheels. He thought it meant they were sure to go over the wall. The scene after the accident, he said, was lamentable.

LIST OF THE INJURED

The three injured detained in hospital were:-

Patrick Lynch (40), driver of the bus, residing at 6 Park Crescent, Dumbarton-shock.

Annie McIntyre or Hannah, 43 Alclutha Avenue, Dumbarton-dislocation of left elbow, fracture of left wrist, and bruise on the hip.

Michael McFall (47), brass dresser, 17 Levenhaugh Street, Dumbarton-injury to right leg and cut on right side of head.

Passengers who were first treated at the hospital and afterwards allowed to go home were:-

William Casey (27), plater's helper, 8 Burn Street, Renton-head injuries.

Edith Jamieson or Easdale (29), 16 Dalhousie Street, Glasgow-injury to left eye, shock, and bruises.

Duncan McArthur (32), marine engineer, Shandon-head injuries.

Peter Haig (18), apprentice ship's officer, Rhuvale, Silverton Avenue, Dumbarton-injuries to head and hands.

George Henry Duncan (26), labourer, 1162 Argyle Street, Glasgow-leg injuries.

John Smith (32), engineer, 37 Random Street, Alexandria-injuries to left leg and left wrist.

Mrs Smith-bruises on body and legs.

Minnie Gillies, Dunbritton Road, Dumbarton-cuts on hands and arm, and compressed throat.

Margaret Dunlop, machinist, Dumbuck Village-cuts to wrists and hands.

Angus McKay (14), 4 Geils Avenue, Dumbarton-cut to left hand.

Thomas Wood (23), engineer, 133 Glasgow Road, Dumbarton-injury to left shoulder.

Andrew Pitt (45), labourer, 136 Crosslet Road, Dumbarton-cut on mouth and injuries to thigh and back.

Ebenezer Hartley (36), hammerman, 120 High Street, Dumbarton-injuries to right shoulder and arm injuries.

Elizabeth McGrory, 123 West Bridgend, Dumbarton-hand injuries.

Jeanie Banks, 5 Beechwood Terrace, Dumbarton-shock.

The following complained of injuries but were able to proceed to their homes:-

A. Simpson, 3 Inchinnan Road, Renfrew-shock and bruises.

Miss Rae H. Grant, 36 Bell Street Renfrew-bruises on arm and side and shock.

Samuel Morgan (47), dancing master, 4 Eastfield Terrace, Dumbarton-shock.

Cecilia Harden or Morgan-shock and injuries to head.

William Brownlee (36), labourer, 1 Levenview Terrace, Dumbarton-shock and scratches on face.

John Henderson (30), riveter, 78 Levenhaugh Street, Dumbarton-injuries to left thumb and right hand, and elbow sprained.

Mrs Henderson-shock and injuries to forehead.

Annie Donaldson or Watson, 105 Douglas Street, Partick-sprained left leg.

Annie Thomson or McIntyre, 83 Cardross Street, Dennistoun, Glasgow-bruises on left side of head, and shock.

Hugh Short, (33), warehouseman, Glasgow-shock.

Henry Woodbridge, nurseryman, Milton Nursery-injuries to right arm.

Annie Graham, hosiery worker, 25 William Street, Dumbarton-shock.

John Bishop, Main Street, Jamestown-shock.

Mrs Bishop-shock.

James McEwan (17), 1 Rockview Terrace, Dumbarton-head injuries.

Mary Miller, 1 Rockview Terrace, Dumbarton-shock and bruises on face.

Geraldine Miller, 1 Rockview Terrace, Dumbarton-bruises on shoulder, arm and legs.

Rev. Matthew Andrew, North U.F. Manse, Dumbarton-cut on hand.

Alexander Hodge, Castlegreen Terrace-head injury.

Andrew Cochrane, Castlegreen Terrace-shock.

Mrs Woodbridge, Dumbuck-shock.

Jane Woodbridge, Dumbuck-bruises on face.

Alexander Fulton, 12 Silverton Avenue-bruises on cheek and leg.

Walter Smith, 5 Beechwood Terrace-head injury.

Robert Lyons, 3 Beechwood Terrace-head and back injury.

Alexander Hutcheon, 28 Silverton Avenue-injury to right hip.

Jean Hutcheon, 28 Silverton Avenue-head injury.

Alexander Gibson, 2 Levengrove Terrace-arm injury, slight shock.

Margaret Deignan (conductress of bus), 18 Risk Street-bruises on legs, body, and head, and shock.

John Stevenson, 10 Victoria Street-leg injuries and ruptured muscles.

MICK SPEAKING

There is a chance that these sayings actually came from Mick himself.

Da's Deid
Once Mick went to the employment exchange, and was asked all his particulars, including his father's name, age and occupation. When asked his father's age, Mick replied:
"If God spares him, by this time next year he'll be ten years deid."

Window Wise
A couple were fighting out the back, so Mick opened his window and shouted to the man to lay off the woman:
Man: "You come doon an ah'll gie ye the same!"
Mick: "Ah widnae come doon if ye gied me twice as much!"

The Poke
A group were giving each other conundrums, and Mick was stuck for one. Eventually he said to one of the group:
"If ye can tell me how many buns is in this poke, ah'll gie ye a' three o them."

Right Enough
There was a crowd of men at Dalreoch Toll one time when, to end an argument, somebody said:
"Ach, tae hell wi it a'! We're a' Jock Tamson's bairns."
Mick: "No at a'! Mah faither wiz cried McFall!"

The Parrot
Friend: "Can your parrot talk, Mick?"
Mick: "Aye, but some days it disnae talk fur months."

Eggsactly
Mick, on being shown some exceptionally large hen eggs, commented:
"Man, it widnae tak mony o thae tae mak a dozen!"

THE WIFE AN WEANS

Blackpool Honeymoon

Newly married, Mick and his young wife went to honeymoon in Blackpool. It was now evening and the young bride was soon in bed while Mick stood looking out the window admiring Blackpool Tower.

Wife: "Mick, ah'm cauld."

Mick: "Don't worry. There's an extra blanket in the wardrobe."

Soon the young bride was tucked in more cosily.

Wife: "Mick, ah'm still cauld."

Mick: "Right, ah'll get ye a hot water bottle."

Wife: "Mick! When ah wiz a wee lassie an wiz cauld, mah maw used tae come in beside me."

Mick: "If ye think ah'm gaun a' the way tae Dumbarton fur yer mother, ye've another think comin!"

A Happily Married Man

Mick was coming along the road one night with his wife, going to the pictures. He bumped into one of his pals from work.

Mick: "Here Tommy Beckett!"

Tommy came up to them and greeted Mick.

Mick: "Hey, Tommy! Ye've never met the wife, huv ye?"

Tommy: "No."

Tommy shook Mrs McFall's hand.

Tommy: "Pleased tae meet ye, Mrs McFall."

Mick: "God, ye're awfa easy pleased, Tommy!"

Mrs McFall's Chandelier

Mick and his wife had just moved house. The new residence was pleasant and a considerable improvement. Mrs McFall had visions of ornamentation regardless of cost.

Mrs McFall: "Mick, this parlour's awfa nice. Ah think it could dae wi a chandelier."

Mick: "There'll be nae chandelier brought in here. Naebody in the hoose could play it!"

Enlightenment

Mick was carrying a grandfather clock down the street one night when a policeman stopped him.

Policeman: "What are you doing with that clock?"

Mick: "A' the lights are oot at hame, sae ah'm cairryin the clock oot tae the street lamp tae see whit time it is."

Sexual Prowess

Mick was digging a hole at the side of the Renton road when a mate came along.

Mate: "Whit are ye daein?"

Mick: "Ah'm gaun oot wi a humfy-backit wummin the night."

Fire

Mick lived in a third-floor tenement flat. One night a spark leapt from the smouldering coals, and soon the parlour carpet was ablaze. Mick and the wife woke up.

Mick: "Gaud, we're on fire! Quick - get oorsels oot tae the stair, an pit the valuables oot the windae."

Wife: "But that's the weddin china ye're thrawin oot!"

Mick: "Ach, it's tae delicate tae cairry doon the stair, ye might trip an break it."

A Mother's Love
Mick was prowling about the stalls at the Barras in Glasgow when he picked up a second-hand wall mirror.

Mick (to himself): "God! That's a photograph of a man hellava like mah faither!"

Mick (to Stallholder): "Could ye wrap that up. Ah want tae gie it tae mah mither fur a present."

When he got home he told his mother that he'd found a picture of someone like his father.

Mother (opening the package and looking at the mirror):
  "That's nothin like yer faither! It's merr like some auld whore fae Glesga!"

The Elegant Dresser
Wee Willie next door died. The day after the funeral his wife came round.

Willie's wife: "Here, Mrs McFall. Here a couple o suits an a couple o shairts an a tie o Willie's. They're tae guid fur the ragman."

That night Mrs McFall caught Mick and got him to try them on. Five minutes later Mick came back.

Mick: "Thae suits are beauties. But they're a wee bit tae tight roon the chest."

Mrs McFall: "An whit aboot the shairts? "

Mick: "Aw, they're jist a wee bit tae tight an a'. Anither hauf inch in the collar wid huv done me fine."

Mrs McFall: "That's jist tae bad. Well, at least the tie'll still dae ye a turn."

Mick: "Aw naw. Ah've went an thrawn that oot. If the suits an shairts didna fit, there's nae way that tie wid !"

Mah Mither's Son

In a pub in Clydebank Mick was chatting to one of the locals.

Local: "Mick, mah mither has a son an it's no me."

Mick: "That's impossible."

Local: "Naw it's no. He's mah brither."

Mick thought that a 'good one' and a few days later, when in a Dumbarton pub, decided to try out the teaser for himself.

Mick: "Mah mither's got a son an it's no me."

Friend: "That's easy, Mick, it's yer brither."

Mick: "Naw, ye're wrang! It's a man up in Clydebank!"

Démenage

Mick was struggling with a wardrobe over Dumbarton Bridge, and fair falling all over the place. A police car then pulled up.

Polis: "Are ye a' right wi that, Mick."

Mick: "Aye, ah'm a' right; the wife's inside cairryin the coats."

Maternity for Eternity

Coming up the brae Mick was telling his mates about his wife having recently given birth.

Fellow: "Are ye...wull ye be huvin a drink?"

Mick: "Whit'll we use fur money?"

Fellow: "Ye'll get maternity benefit, see."

Mick: "Wull ah?"

Fellow: "Aye, it'll be up tae you tae gae doon an get the maternity benefit."

So Mick went down to the office and went up to the girl at the desk.

Girl: "Well, Sir, what can I do for you?"

Mick: "Ah want mah eternity money."

Girl: "But eternity means hereafter."

Mick: "Aye, it's that ah'm here efter."

The DIY Man

Mick was standing on the kitchen table painting the ceiling when his wife came in.

Mrs McFall: "Ye'll need tae pit a newspaper doon."

Mick: "Nae need, ah can reach fine the way ah am."

Wallpapering

During the Depression when out of work Mick's pal asked him what they would do that day.

Mick: "Jist come doon an ah'll show ye mah hoose. Ah've been daein a bit o paperin."

His mate admired his work.

Pal: "It's nae bad, but what the hell's a' thae lumps?"

Mick: "Did ye think ah'd gae tae a' the bother o takin the pictures doon!"

Give You My Last Penny

Mick was at home in front of the fire, toasting his feet. His wife was getting ready to go out.

Mrs McFall: "Here's me huvin tae gae oot in this rain wi mah shoes leakin, an you sittin there in front o the fire."

Mick: "Well, ah'll gie ye a lane o mah shoes, an ah'll see if ah can stick it oot here."

A Strangled Choke

Mrs McFall had insisted Mick get a new scarf, so he eventually did, and came home with it on, a gairish, Fair Isle kind of one.

Mrs McFall: "Aw Mick, that's dreadful lookin! It really disnae suit. Ye'll jist huv tae tak it back."

But Mick had taken ages picking it, and besides he was too embarrassed to go back. But the wife's advice prevailed, and he eventually did.

Mick: "Hello, here again! Ye'll need tae tak this scarf back."

Assistant: "But you seemed quite pleased with it earlier."

Mick: "Aye, well...er...but when ah got back tae the hoose wi it, ah found it wiz far tae tight."

MICK JOINS UP

Paternity

During World War I Mick, while serving in the trenches, received a telegram informing him that his wife had just had a baby. Congratulations all round - but one man looked thoughtful.

Man: "When did ye last huv leave. Mick?"

Mick: "Mair nor a year ago."

Man: "Then ye've got tae face it. Mick. It's no your wean."

Mick: "How no? There's six years between mah brither an me!"

A Conscientious Reporter

In World War I Mick joined the Signals. and the sergeant got the new recruits together.

Sergeant: "Now I want someone to look after the carrier pigeons. Anyone with experience?"

Silence!

Sergeant: "Well then. any volunteers?"

Mick: "Aye, ah'll huv a go."

A few hours later a bird was seen arriving.

Sergeant: "Look. man, there's a bird now."

Mick: "Right. ah'll awa an get the message."

Five minutes later.

Sergeant: "Well, then. McFall. have you got the message? "

Mick: "Aye, sir. the bird went coo...coo."

All Clear

Mick was a bomb aimer in the RAF. After one particularly hazardous mission Mick's plane taxied down ahead of the other planes in the squadron. At the crew's debriefing Mick was asked how he had come back with a full bomb rack.

Mick: "Well, ah wiz ower the target and jist aboot tae press the release when, a' of a sudden, the "a' clear" sounded, so ah knew there was nae need tae drap the bombs."

The Civilian War Effort

During the Second World War purchased articles were frequently unwrapped owing to the shortage of paper. Mick had a job assisting a fishmonger. A rather coarse woman entered the shop and planked a chamber pot on the counter.

Coarse woman: "A pound o fillet!"

Mick (banging a pound note down on the counter): "A pound ye don't."

Lights Out

During World War II a searchlight was located on Castlehill. During one of the 1941 air raids the light actually picked up an enemy plane.

Light Operator: "Jist run up that light an gie the pilot a doin."

Mick: "Ye're no catchin me oot wi that yin. Ah know you. When ah'm hauf way up ye'll switch the light oot!"

The Flair

Mick was on a bombing raid over Germany, working in the bomb bay. The pilot's voice came over the intercom.

Pilot: "Target coming up. Visibility poor. Prepare to drop flare."

Mick (to navigator): "Nae way! Ah'm no goin tae fa oot o this aircraft, are you?"

Rommel's Foe

Pat and Mick were in the desert with the 8th Army.

Pat: "Ah widnae mind bein in the Vale the day!"
Mick: "How's that?"
Pat: "It's the day o the Cattle Show."
Mick: "Well, they're gettin rerr weather fur it!"

And they Came to Pass

Mick was on sentry duty with the Home Guard at a road block on the Renton road. It was a dark night, and a young married couple approached, totally unaware of Mick's presence.

Mick   (suddenly stepping out from behind the barrier):
        "Halt! Who goes therr?"
Couple (frightened out of their wits):
        "Oh! Jesus, Mary an Joseph!"
Mick: "Pass, The Holy Family! "

Boats

Mick went along to join the Navy, and the recruiting officer took down details.

Officer: "Can you swim? "

Mick: "How? Huv ye nae boats? "

Going Home

Mick passed the interview for a job in the Faslane Submarine Base.

Employer: "On starting would three weeks' lying time be O.K?"

Mick: "Naw, it's a' right."

Employer: "Do you need a sub, a cash advance ?"

Mick: "Naw, ah'll tak the bus hame."

THE TRAVELLING MAN

There and Back
Mick was walking to Cardross. There was a hellava gale blowing. He tried to light his pipe, but couldn't because of the way the wind was blowing. To shelter the pipe bowl, he was forced to turn around. He never got to Cardross. When his pipe was lit he just carried on walking, forgetting to turn round again.

The Home Lover
Mick wasn't used to travelling. The first time he used a bus he was in a state of uncertainty when the conductor came up to him.

Mick: "Ah want a return ticket."
Conductor: "Where to?"
Mick: "Tae Dumbarton of course! Where else wud ah be returnin tae?"

Up the Toon
Mick was in Glasgow. He'd gone up on the bus, the only way he'd ever gone to Glasgow. He transacted his business and went back to the bus station, to find a notice saying that the buses were on strike. Forced to get the train, Mick was told to go to the booking office window for a ticket. There he joined a queue with a couple of women ahead of him. Mick was still wondering what to say when he heard the women buying their tickets.

First woman: "Maryhill, single."
Second woman: "Bellahouston, single."
Mick: "Mick McFall, mairrit wi two weans."

One-Man Buses
When it was decided to dispense with bus conductors and conductresses, 'clippies', buses so manned were soon referred to as one-man buses. Mick and a friend stood at a bus stop.
Friend: "This is a wan-man bus, Mick."
Mick: "You get on then an I'll catch the next wan."

Taken for a Ride
Mick was intrigued by the new one-man buses and climbed up on to the top deck for the ride. No sooner had the bus set off however than he raced down stairs and shot off the bus. He was picked up by a man who knew him.
Friend: "You O.K.,Whit's wrang?"
Mick: "Thae new buses - they've nae driver!"

Personal Hygiene
Clippie: "You fartit?"
Mick: "Naw."
Clippie: "Gaud, it's hummin! You sure ye've no fartit ?"
Mick: "Certain."
Clippie, turning away, giving her final verdict, *sub voce*:
"Ye must huv shat yersel then."
Mick: "Noo ye're talkin!"

The Post-Decimalisation Traveller
Mick was coming home from a night out and waiting for a bus, but none came. So he thought he'd go home in style and waved down a taxi.
Mick: "Up tae Castlehill, please."
On arrival...
Cab Driver: "That'll be a pound fifty."
Mick: "Aw, ah've only got a pound. Ah'll tell ye whit. Drive me back tae the station an ah'll walk it fae therr."

The Rotten Musician
Mick was on the Garelochhead-Helensburgh bus, sitting next to two
good-looking young women, when the conductress came up:
   Brunette: " Two tae Rhu."
   Mick: " Tra La La."

Ah'll Tak the High Road
Pat and Mick had a heated argument over the quickest route from
Dumbarton to Helensburgh. Pat claimed it was by the A814 road,
Mick was convinced it was by rail. Eventually they decided to settle
the issue in a practical way, with Pat walking the road and Mick
walking along the railway line. They set off together from Dumbarton
Central railway station, and in due course Pat arrived in Helensburgh
where, after several hours, he still had not seen Mick appear. Next day
Pat saw Mick coming down the Cardross road:
   Pat: "Hey, whit fur did ye no turn up at Helensburgh?"
   Mick: "Never mind a' that! Jist you wait till ah find oot who changed
      thae railway points at Dalreoch!"

Trawling Trouble

Mick and his brother were out on a boat on Loch Lomond fishing. For ages they got nothing, so they eventually moved along a couple of hundred yards. Still nothing. After a further hour they moved close inshore and must have come over a run of salmon. Within half an hour the boat was near gunwhale-deep in fish. They made back for Balloch.

Mick: "Aw, we'll mak a killin here. We'll be able tae sell these salmon tae the hotels doon at Balloch."

Brother: "Did ye notice where we got thae fish, so we can come back ?"

Mick: "Aye. ah decided tae mak sure o it. Ah made a mark on the side o the boat efter we'd hauled in."

Brother: "Aw, ye mug ye. There's nae guarantee we'll get the same boat the morra night when we come back!"

Bella Lost At Bellahouston
Mick went up to the 1938 Empire Exhibition with his old auntie Bella, and in the crowds they got separated. The wireless was still comparatively in its infancy at the time and devoted a lot of its broadcasting to the news and weather. All Mick could hear from a loudspeaker was :

"Anticyclone over Europe."

Mick: "Holy God, the auld bitch! Ah never knew she could gae a bike!"

Fame At Last

Later that day at Bellahouston Park. Mick finally got round to the famous giraffe-necked women from Africa, only to find the shows closing.

Mick: "Aw, jist hang on a sec, ah'm workin a' week. Jist tell the girls it's Mick McFall, the Go As You Please Man fae Dumbarton."

Showman: "O.K.,....hey right enough! These girls are jist dyin tae see you! They've heard a' aboot you in Masobutoland!"

THE MAN ABOUT TOWN

Green Blues

Mick applied to join the Dumbarton "Big Green" bowling club, but got a letter back refusing his application, no reason given.

> Mick: "Och, well. That's no sae bad. Ah wudnae want tae be a member o a club that hud me as a member anyhow."

The Rich Man

Mick and his pal were going along the street when Mick saw a penny and picked it up. The two of them carried on and crossed Dumbarton Bridge when, all of a sudden, Mick tossed the coin into the Leven.

> Pal: "Whit're ye throwin awa money like that fur?"
> Mick: "Aw, it's no worth tuppence."

The Green Philosopher

Mick was with a friend contemplating the new traffic lights on the Cardross road:

> Friend: "Hey, that's magic! See that red light though. Ye're supposed tae stap."
> Mick: "But how dae they know there's any traffic tae stap?"

A Nod and a Wink

Mick and his pal were outside the Black Bull in West Bridgend.

> Mick: "Hey, ah'm gaun tae mak a fool o that barman. Ah'll tell him a tall story, an when ah wink, you nod.

Inside the pub.

> Mick (to the barman, winking at his pal):
> "A double whisky, an it's on that fella therr!"

The Patient

Mick was told by the doctor to bring a sample of urine. He came into the surgery with a pail full of urine.

Doctor: "Surely to goodness you didn't carry that down the road!"

Mick: "Naw, ah didnae. Ah came on the bloody bus wi it."

The Provost's Farewell

Crowds of people lined the High Street as the funeral procession of a local dignitary went by. A stranger, passing through the town, turned to Mick.

Stranger: "Do you know whose funeral this is by any chance?"

Mick: "Nae idea. Right enough though, ah expect it'll be the fellah in the box's."

Self-Destruct Button

Mick was going down a dark alley when he got jumped on by five youths. They could only get threepence out of him.

Oldest youth: "O.K., man. Only 3p. What are you struggling for?"

Mick: "Ah thought ye were gaun fur the five pounds that's in mah sock."

Lighting Sense

Mick's found crawling about in the house by his wife.

Mrs McFall: "Whit are ye daein on the flair?"

Mick: "Ah lost a hauf croon."

Mrs McFall: "Whereabouts did ye lose it?"

Mick: "Oot in the street."

Mrs McFall: "Well, whit are ye lookin fur it in here fur?"

Mick: "There's mair light in here."

Right Enough
Mick was walking down West Bridgend when he bumped into his mate Jimmy.

Mick: "Ah'm no sure if ah need tae sign on the day. Huv ye got the day's date?"

Jimmy: "Naw. But jist look at the newspaper in yer pocket."

Mick: "That's nae use. It's yesterday's!"

A Man of His Word
Mick was visiting his farm labourer pal Tam who was working up on Dumbarton Muir at Garshake. Darkness fell early, and it was clear a storm was brewing.

Mick: "Ah'd better be aff. It'll be a lang road in this weather."

Tam: "Here, tak this torch tae show ye the path. But mind, ah want it back."

About one o'clock in the morning there was a loud banging on the bothy door. Tam, thinking some poor soul had got lost on the moor, stumbled in the hurry to open up the door.

Tam: "Laud! Who's that?"

Mick: "It's me - Mick! Here's yer torch back."

Nae Ba'room
Mick bought a pair of trousers from Bald's the tailors in Dumbarton High Street, but when he tried them on again at home he found they were too tight around the crutch. Next day when he went back to the shop he was embarrassed to see a young girl was serving.

Girl: "Good day Sir, can I help you."

Mick: "Oo...er...these troosers, ah bought them yesterday an...er... oh...aye, ah went ba'room dancin in them last night at the Rialto."

Girl: "But the Rialto's a cinema, there's no ballroom there!"

Mick: "Aye, well...er...that's whit ah'm tryin tae tell ye..."

Strung Up

A policeman was walking down the High Street late one night, suddenly looking up when he sensed a strange shape illuminated in a street light. There was a man, hanging upside down, his bootlace attached to the lamp.

Policeman: "Whit are ye daein, Mick?"
Mick: "Ah'm gaun tae commit suicide."
Policeman: "How are ye gaun tae commit suicide like that? Ye might've pit the lace roon yer neck!"
Mick: "Ah tried that, but ah nearly choked."

The Hunter

Mick went along to a shop in the High Street, which had a great window display centred around an owl, was greatly impressed and went inside.

Mick: "Wull ye gie me that bird in the windae?"
Assistant: "Oh, that's a night owl."
Mick: "Ah don't gie a damn if it's a fortnight aul'. Ah could dae wi a bird fur the pot."

Schoolpals

Mick was relaxing in a pub when the barman approached him and placed a wee hauf an a hauf pint before him.

Mick: "Ah didnae order that."
Barman: "That man ower there said tae gie it tae ye fur auld time's sake."
Mick: "Whit man?"
Barman: "That man wi the bald heid an moustache. Says he wiz at school wi ye."
Mick: "There must be some mistake, there wiz naebody wi a bald heid an moustache at school wi me!"

THE WORKING MAN

The Manitoba Mallet Man

Mick was boasting to his pals about a period he had spent in Canada working on a cattle ranch.

Mick: "Ah wiz sent tae fence aff a hunner miles o prairie. In the mornin ah hammert in the first post an hung mah jaicket on it. Ah worked that hard that, by dinner time, it took me three days tae gae back and get mah piece oot mah pocket!"

Nut for Starters

Mick was among a crowd of men at the top of Dennystown Brae when word got round that they were starting a lot of men at Denny's the Shipbuilders' yard. So Mick went down to the yard and found that men were getting started right enough, but no one came up to see him. So he went back to the men hanging around at the top of Dennystown Brae.

Men: "How did ye no get a start, Mick?"

Mick: "Ah don't know. They were startin men right and left."

Man: "How come you didnae get a start then?"

Mick: "Ah wiz placed right in the middle."

The Honest Drover

Mick was driving two cows over Bonhill Bridge on his way to the market.

Passer-by (knowing Mick was always good for a laugh):
"Hey, Mick, gie's wan o yer coos!"

Mick: "Ah canna, they're a' coonted!"

Thrown on the Broo

Mick finally got a job besides his pal in Denny's. They went down one day to the yard, and found it closed. A notice on the gate explained that the yard had gone into liquidation and the receiver had been called in. The journey home brought them past a group of protesters whose banners summarised the inevitable effects of the closure. Mick was clearly drawn into the general mood of despair and on crossing the Leven bridge he took his dinner piece out of his pocket and threw it into the river.

Mate: "Whit did ye dae that fur, Mick?"

Mick: "Well, ye saw the heidlines, nae work, nae chuck."

Found - Out !

Mick was working in Hardie and Gordon's foundry at Dalreoch when a spate of thefts started. One day Mick was walking out of the main gate with his wheel barrow.

Gateman: "Hey - wait on! Whit's that blacksmith's anvil daein in yer barra?"

Mick: "Aw jings - ye cannae expect me tae check every load ah'm takin oot!

Take A Seat

Mick, on the broo, went into the employment exchange.

Mick: "Ah'm lookin fur a job."

Clerk: "Go and take a seat."

Mick went away and reappeared a long time later.

Mick: "Ah've no got a job yet - but ah'm makin a wee fortune sellin these seats."

Lavatorial Humour

Mick was working at Denny's. He was down at the quay when a work mate came over to him.

Worker: "Hey. Mick. whaur's the urinal?"

Mick: "Ah think it's that yin wi the three funnels ower therr!"

The Eclectic Drinker

Mick had a temporary job as a debt collector. He was about to go into a close in College Street when a man, lounging against the close wall, stopped him.

Man: "Ah widna gae up that close. There's a case o VD up there."
Mick: "It's O.K., pal. Ah can drink anything."

The Man of Letters

Mick was in a pub one night and fell into conversation with two or three fellahs who were arguing as to which of them had the hardest job.

Coalminer: "Mine's the hardest, workin in cramped conditions an a' that."

Foundry worker:"Aw, naw. Workin in swelterin heat like ah huv tae. Ah've tae wear eighteen jerseys tae keep the heat fae searin me."

Mick: "Ah've got a harder job than that."
Men: "Whit dae you dae?"
Mick: "Ah'm a postman."
Men (falling about laughing): "A postman! How the blazes is being a postman a hard job."
Mick: "Ah cannae read."

Front to Back

Mick was working in Denny's shipyard and, having slept in, was late for work. He was quite concerned about the prospects of being locked out from his morning shift and losing a half day's pay. In the rush to get dressed he happened to put his trousers on front to back. Somehow he reached his workplace on time but on dashing up a makeshift gang-plank he fell headlong into the poorly-lit hold of the partially-built ship.

Work mate: "Gosh! Are ye a' right Mick?"

Mick was quite dazed but had escaped serious injury. In picking himself up almost immediately however he noticed, in the process of dusting himself down, that something wasn't quite right.

Mick: "Aye, ah seem tae be O.K., but ah've no hauf gied mahsel a hellava bad twist."

His Darker Side

During the Depression of the early Thirties Mick, after much tiring walking, managed to get an unskilled job in Paisley. The early morning start and the long working hours would make daily travelling to and from work prohibitive, so further weary perambulations were necessary to find digs he could afford. Finally he was successful. But:

Landlady: "Ye'll huv tae share the room wi a nigger, but."

Mick: "Nae problem. Ah'm that tired ah could sleep wi a pig!"

However, Mick's propensity for stupidity was well known, even in Paisley, and that night while he was asleep they blackened his face. No doubt the negro was enjoying the joke as much as anyone.

Next morning, having been deliberately wakened late, he had no time for normal ablutions. Rushing down the road he saw his reflection in a shop window and exclaimed:

"Good God! They've wakened the wrang man."

Tango. Foxtrot

Mick and Tim Martin got a job as painters, and went to do a job at Ballantine's Distillery, a tall building, six or seven storeys high.

Foreman: "Would you please red lead the name off the sign board at the top of the building. There's a war on."

Mick: "Ye don't want a red leider; ye want a squadron leader!"

(This joke, like many, has variants - e.g. there were no more ships on the stocks at Denny's so Mick was asked to red lead a crane).

The Forward Thinker

Mick was a binman, a 'scaffie'. One morning he came up to his foreman.

Mick: "Can ah get awa early the day? The wife an I are aff tae a waddin."

Foreman: "Well...right, seein as ye're a good timekeeper, an it's Friday, ye can awa at three an ah'll write ye in fur four."

But Mick nipped off at dinner time, and came back at one, with a new suit on and hair gleaming. But the foreman saw him return.

Foreman: "Hey, you! Huv you nipped hame already? Ah said at three."

Mick: "Aye, ah know ye did. But ah jist remembered, we've tae be at the waddin fur four, an that's ower neat. This way, all ah've got tae dae is nip back hame and change mah simmet!"

Dropped a Brick

Mick was working on a building site.

Foreman: "Awa and get a wheelbarra an shift thae bricks!"

Mick returned about a minute later with a wheel barrow.

Foreman: "Hey there's nae bottom in that barra!"

Mick: "Aye, right enough. But that maks it a hellava lot easier tae push!"

On The Buses

After a considerable period of unemployment Mick finally got a job as a bus driver. Wearing his new uniform he proudly set off from Glasgow on the Balloch run. As he progressed along the road he became increasingly aware of people standing at the kerbside waving him to stop. Ignoring their gestures, Mick said to himself.

"Aye! they're a' wavin at me noo!

They didnae dae much wavin when ah wiz idle!"

On Reflection

Mick, working with a removal firm, was carrying a large mirror downstairs out to the van. He suddenly saw his reflection and let the mirror go. The mirror crashed down the stairs and shattered as it hit the floor.

Boss: "Whit the hell did ye dae that fur?"

Mick: "There wiz nae use the two o us cairryin it!"

Cheesed Off

Mick had just finished the morning's work and it was time for his
dinner piece - there were no canteens in those days. When he was
taking his tea he opened up his piece.

Mick: "Aw, bloody cheese! Cheese again."

And then he threw his piece to the seagulls.

Mate: "Aw...why did ye throw...dae ye no like cheese?"

Mick: "Aye, it a' right, but ah had cheese yesterday, an cheese the
day before."

Next day Mick opened his piece again and looked desparingly at it.

Mick: "Och, cheese again. This'll no hauf get ye doon!"

Mate: "Why don't ye tell the wife ye're no happy Mick, an get her
tae pit something else in yer piece noo an again?"

Mick: "Aye, that's the trouble. The wife's in hospital jist noo.
Ah'm makin up mah ain pieces."

A Working Man Needs His Piece

Mick's wife is out of hospital, and makes his pieces again. He comes
home that night.

Mrs McFall: "How wiz yer piece then, Mick?"

Mick: "Well, er, ye know ah always like bread an butter an
cheese. But, eh...it's a new job ah'm on, an...wan
slice, well, it's no enough."

The next day Mick opens his pieces box... and there's two slices of
bread. When he gets home...

Mrs McFall: "Well, how wiz yer pieces the day, Mick?"

Mick: "Well, er, no bad, but it's a right heavy job ah'm on.
Ah could dae wi mair nor a couple o slices."

Next day there are three slices in Mick's piece box.

"An how wiz yer piece the day?" inquired his wife
when he got home. "Nae complaints this time ah
hope."

Mick: "Well, O.K., ah suppose, but ah wiz still kin o hungry
            a' aifternoon."
Right, says his wife to herself that night. That's enough! I'm sick of
his complaining! So she gets out a loaf and splits it down the middle,
gets out about half a pound of butter and spreads it on, sticks a big
half-pound wedge of cheese in the middle, clamps it all together,
wraps it up with string and sticks it in his dinner poke.
Come next evening, and the wife is ready for him.
    Mrs McFall: "Well, Mick, an how wiz yer piece the day then?"
    Mick: "Aye, well, that wiz mair like a workin man's meal...
                but ah see ye're back tae wan slice again."

The Way to a Man's Heart
Mick got a job in a sewage works. One day it was very hot, and Mick
was walking along with his jacket slung over his shoulder. Suddenly
the jacket slipped off his shoulder, into a large pool of sewage. Mick
started climbing down towards his jacket.
    Mate: "Mick, whit are ye daein? Ye're no tryin tae get yer jaicket
            fae there noo, are ye!"
    Mick: "Naw, ah'm no tryin tae get mah jaicket! Ah'm tryin tae
            get the pieces that are in mah pocket!"

Rings a Bell
Walking down the street, Mick saw a familiar face.
    Mick: "Hey, how are ye daein?"
    Fellow: "Sorry, dae ah know you?"
    Mick: "Aye, surely ye remember me, Mick McFall?"
    Fellow: "Naw, sorry. Never seen ye afore."
    Mick: "But ah'm sure ah worked wi you in Greenock."
    Fellow: "Naw, never been there in mah life."
    Mick: "Well, it must've been two other fellas that were working
            together in Scott's!"

Anchor Aweigh

After a number of years in employment on building sites, Mick gets a job in a shipyard. On his first day there the foreman directs him to assist a squad of men who are busy fitting the ship's anchor chains. His pal meets up with him at the tea-break and asks how he likes the new job.

Mick: "Ah don't think ah'll be stayin in this job tae long."

Pal: "How, whit's wrang?"

Mick: "It looks like they expect ye tae work like the devil here; ye should see the size o the picks up therr on the front o that ship.

GONE TO THE DOGS

Dog Lovers

Mick and his brother bought two greyhounds from a pal who was leaving the area. They had a chicken run on their plot, and decided to keep the dogs there. So they went up and penned the animals in and were walking home when it occurred to them that they ought to have identified each other's dogs so they could tell whose was whose the next day. So they went back to the hut and, looking round, saw a pair of shears.

Mick: "Ah'll cut a bit aff the tail o mine so's we'll know it.
         Mine'll be the dug wi a short tail."

So Mick clipped the tail and the two brothers made for the door. Just then the other dog made a breenge for the door. They managed to close the door in time but the dog got its tail trapped, and the tip came off, which kind of nullified their efforts.

Mick: "Wait a minute. Gie us thae shears
         again. Ah'll just mak a wee 'V'
         in the dug's ear. Noo don't let
         yours get its heid caught in the
         door fur God's sake!"

They carried out the operation and were just
going down the road quite pleased with
themselves, when another thought struck Mick's
brother.

Brother: "We're a couple o mugs. We didnae
         need tae cut the dug's ear at a'."
Mick: "How no?"
Brother: "Sure the black yin's bigger than the white yin!"

The Twa Dugs

Mick was coming home drunk. "God," he thought, "the wife said she'll kill me if ah came hame drunk like this again." So he decided upon securing a peace offering for his wife, and remembered a neighbour's dog had just had pups which they were trying to get rid of, and his wife had said that she'd fancied one.

Arriving at the neighbour's, Mick was told that there were just two left, and why didn't he take both? A good idea, Mick thought, and set off home.

Outside the house, now somewhat soberer, Mick thought himself a bit of a coward and decided to see how he would get on meeting his wife without the dogs, and laid them down on the step in the basket he'd been given.

Another neighbour saw this move and decided to play a trick on Mick, and took the puppies from underneath the blanket. Meanwhile Mick's well intended plan was going wrong, and he was now getting hell from his wife, so he said, in retreating:

"Jist a minute, hen, dinnae be sae mad. Ah've got a wee something here fur ye."

Mick brought the basket from the step and lifted the blanket to discover there was nothing there.

"Aw, hell," he said. "The wan's went an ate the ither!"

Jobby Trouble

Mick was complaining to his workmates about his wee dog which consistently did its business under the living room sofa. One day his pals asked him if he had finally trained the animal.

Mick: "Aye, ah've solved the problem!"
Pals: "Whit way?"
Mick: "Ah've cut the legs aff the sofa!"

Anither Twa Dugs

Mick went up to Glasgow Market, and got the chance of two grey-
hound pups. When he got out the train at Dalreoch he realised that he
didn't have much time left for a drink at the Springbank, so he nipped
home extra quick and handed the pups in to his wife.

Mick:	"Here ye are - gie them something tae eat, they're
	bound tae be hungry."

A wee while later he was back at the house.

Mick:	"Well, how's mah wee beauts?"

Mrs McFall: "Who the hell have you been kiddin on? There wiz
	naethin in that bag!"

Mick:	"Aw, they've been hungry right enough, the wan's ate
	the ither."

The Master Tactician

Mick and his brother bought a dog and took it down to the flapping
track at Boghead. They put all the money they had left from the sale
on it...and it came in last.

Mick:	"Aw, it wiznae the dug's fault. It was drawn on the outside,
	and the track wiz awfa muddy. It jist didnae huv a
	chance."

Brother: "Aye, ye're right there. We'll gie it another chance next
	week."

So they fed it on the best of food all week, took it down to the track,
put all their rent money on it, and again it came in last.

Brother: "Aw, come on now, Mick. Listen, let's face it, it's nae guid.
	We'll huv tae get it pit doon."

Mick:	"Jings! We've nae money left. We canna afford that."

Brother: "Well, how about we jist tie a big stane roon its neck an
	chuck it in the Leven?"

Mick was too much of a dog lover for that, so he pondered a while.

Mick:	"Here, ah've got it! Ah'll tell ye whit we'll dae!
	We'll jist tak it doon tae Havoc Shore, and we'll run awa
	fae it!"

The Bird Table

Mick had a hen run out the Renton road, near the railway. Every time he went out to it there was another hen or two lying dead on the lines.

Mick: "Ah'll need tae dae something aboot this," he thought.
"Damn it, jist the thing!" he said a minute later.

So he went off down to Dalreoch Railway Station and asked for a train time table. He went back and stuck it up in the hut.

Mick: "There's the time o the trains. Noo it's yer ain fault if ye get killt."

Henhoose Capers

Mick arranged with some friends to give him a hand to move his henhouse from one part of the garden to another. At the set time the stalwarts appeared but could see no sign of Mick. One of the group knew where Mick had thought of putting the henhouse, so it was decided that they would set to and move it. After considerable peching and panting they managed to resite the hut on the desired spot. As they wiped their brows the henhouse door opened and Mick stepped out.

Pals: "Whit the devil dae ye think ye're daein in that thing! We've been cairryin ye aboot."
Mick: "Well, somebody hud tae cairry the perches!"

Fair Carried Away

Mick had got permission to site his chicken run Dennystown-Dalmoak way. One January, as ever, the Leven burst its banks and Mick was working in the yard at Denny's when a workmate pointed out the hen coop floating past.

Mick: "It's a'right. Bernie, naebody'll get thae hens. Ah've got the key here in mah pocket."

Houseproud

At an agricultural show Mick won a goat in a raffle. On his return home his wife was dismayed.

Mrs McFall: "We cannae huv that here, Mick!"
Mick: "How no?"
Mrs McFall: "Whit aboot the smell?"
Mick: "Ach. it'll soon get used tae that!"

Beehive Behaviour

Mick was walking past the fountain in Alexandria with a beehive tucked under his arm when a pal stopped him.

Pal: "Whaur are you awa tae wi that?"
Mick: "The Christie Park. There's nae flooers in mah gairden fur the bees tae mak honey wi."
Pal: "Guid idea. But they'll maybe no let ye pit yer hive up among their flooers. Ye're better tae go in at the deid o night, sae as naebody'll see ye"
Mick: "Aye, right enough. But the park's closed at night. Ye're no supposed tae gae in then."

Hardy Horse

Another time there was a big race and Mick asked his pals for a tip, and they gave him one. Going to place a bet he was stopped by a pal who asked him what he'd put his money on, and Mick told him.

    Pal: "That's no worth yer while. It's scratched."

    Mick: "But ah've seen them runnin wi chunks oot o them!"

Gee-Up !

Mick was at a riding school. Someone noticed that he had placed the saddle on the wrong way round.

    Fellow learner: "Hey, Mick! That saddle's pointin tae the horse's arse!"

    Mick (huffishly): "Auch! How dae ye know whit direction ah'm gaun tae go?"

Vague Tipster

Mick had been standing down at the Dalreoch Toll for hours, chatting, largely about the St. Leger, being held that day. He met a fellah on the way up the brae.

Mick: "Whit dae ye fancy fur the big race?"

Fellah: "Ah dunno."

A wee while later, down in the town, he asked another punter:

"Whit dae ye fancy fur Doncaster?"

"Ah dunno," came the reply.

That should do the trick, he thought, and put on a couple of bob. Later that afternoon he saw one of his pals again.

Mick: "Whit won?"

Pal: "Ah dunno."

So Mick shot into the bookie's to claim his winnings.

Bookie: "Whit had ye on?"

Mick: "Ah dunno."

Bookie: "Get the hell oot o here! Ah've too much on mah plate
         tae bother wi the likes o you!"